ESSENTIAL MANAGERS

MANAGING
BUDGETS

STEPHEN BROOKSON

A Dorling Kindersley Book

Dorling **DK** Kindersley

LONDON, NEW YORK, SYDNEY, DELHI, PARIS
MUNICH & JOHANNESBURG

Senior Editor Adèle Hayward
Senior Designer Caroline Marklew
DTP Designer Jason Little
Production Controller Heather Hughes

Senior Managing Editor Stephanie Jackson
Managing Art Editor Nigel Duffield
US Editor Gary Werner

Produced for Dorling Kindersley by

studio **cactus** ⊙

13 SOUTHGATE STREET WINCHESTER HAMPSHIRE SO23 9DZ

Editor Richard Hammond
Designers Helen Bracey, Laura Watson

First published in the United States by
Dorling Kindersley Publishing, Inc.
95 Madison Avenue
New York, New York 10016

First American Edition, 2000

2 4 6 8 10 9 7 5 3 1

CIP data available on request
ISBN 0-7894-5969-8

Reproduced by Colourscan, Singapore
Printed in Hong Kong by Wing King Tong Co. Ltd.

See our complete catalogue at
www.dk.com

CONTENTS

WRITING A BUDGET

MONITORING A BUDGET

INTRODUCTION

The managers most likely to succeed in today's business environment are those who understand how to use budgets as business tools for departmental and personal success. Managing Budgets is an informative and practical guide to the essential skills needed to produce accurate and useful budgets. The three key stages to budgeting – preparing, writing, and monitoring – are clearly explained to help you significantly improve the quality of your budgets. Practical advice is given on how to challenge figures logically and how to monitor procedures sensibly. One hundred and one concise tips scattered throughout the text give further vital information. Finally, a thorough self-assessment exercise allows you to evaluate and improve on your budgeting skills.

UNDERSTANDING BUDGETING

Budgeting is the process of preparing, compiling, and monitoring financial budgets. It is a key management tool for planning and controlling a department within an organization.

WHAT IS A BUDGET?

A budget is a plan for future activities. It can be expressed in a number of ways, but usually it describes all of a business in financial terms. It is the yardstick by which an organization's performance is measured.

> **1** Always remember that if you fail to plan, you are planning to fail.

MANAGEMENT SKILLS ▲
As a manager, you must be able to communicate your budgetary requirements effectively.

DEFINING A BUDGET

A budget is a statement of monetary plans that is prepared in advance of a forthcoming period, usually one year. Budgets are often thought to include only planned revenues and expenditures (the profit-and-loss account), which show the income that each part of an organization is expected to generate and the total cost that it is authorized to incur. However, a budget should also include an organization's plans for assets and liabilities (budgeted balance sheet) and the estimates for cash receipts and payments (budgeted cash flow).

Overall expenditure type is divided into component parts, including a clear description of each cost

A total figure for departmental expenditure types is calculated (this figure is then put into expenditure totals for the whole organization)

MARKETING DEPARTMENT BUDGET YEAR 2		
ADVERTISING EXPENDITURE	YEAR 2 BUDGET	YEAR 1 ACTUAL
Gizmo pre-launch leaflet research	110	100
Gizmo launch Geneva	60	52
TV spring year 2 offensive	700	680
Radio advertisements March year 2	600	554
Newspaper quarter-page monthly	70	63
Stall at Berlin Trade Fair	450	512
Dealer incentive program	60	54
National Trade Body funding	80	90
Stall at Birmingham Trade Fair	40	44
Radio advertisements May year 2	100	67
TV fall year 2 offensive	80	68
TOTALS	2350	2284

Heading gives business department and budget period currently being prepared

Financial amounts anticipated to be spent are presented alongside actual amounts spent in previous period

---

2 Manage your business, do not let it manage you.

QUESTIONS TO ASK YOURSELF

Q Has my organization been budgeting successfully for many years?

Q Did anything go particularly wrong in last year's budgeting?

Q Does the business have any unusual features that will cause budgeting problems?

Q Are there any managers that are particularly good at budgeting?

▲ LISTING A TYPICAL BUDGET
In this example, a marketing department has prepared next year's expenditure budget by listing the activities on which they anticipate spending money, compared with what they spent in the current year.

BUDGETING IN BUSINESS

Using budgets is vital for the planning and control of a business. Budgets help co-ordinate actions of different managers and departments while securing commitment to achieving results. Budgets also give authority for departmental managers to incur expenditure by their department and provide targets for earning revenue.

By providing benchmarks against which actual activities are monitored, budgets are a reliable way of analyzing actual business performance. Budgets are therefore a way for an organization to generate information so that it can measure how it is progressing, and how it might adapt to an agreed business plan in view of actual performance.

WHY BUDGET?

Budgets help an individual, department, and organization achieve planned objectives. Budgets also help to illustrate the financial responsibilites of the organization to several groups of people: lenders, suppliers, employees, customers, and the owners.

3 Use budgets effectively and they will be key tools for success.

RECOGNIZING YOUR RESPONSIBILITIES

While budgetary systems are more common in larger organizations, where sophisticated and formalized management techniques exist, the usefulness of budgeting in smaller organizations is just as great. You must recognize what your personal and departmental responsibilities are to your organization and budget appropriately. The validity and usefulness of a budget depend on the people who put it together. Budgets are only as good as the individuals who prepare them.

Focuses on role in budgeting process

Satisfies the owner's expectations

Puts in maximum effort

Fulfills managerial obligations

Ensures business is successful

▲ **RESPONSIBILITIES FOR BUDGETING**
Just as budgets must achieve a number of aims within an organization, so, as a manager, you must be prepared to fulfill a number of responsibilities as part of the budgeting process.

4 Decide on the role and responsibility of your budget to suit the whole organization.

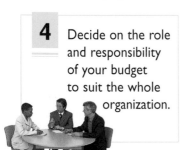

THE ROLE OF BUDGETING

Budgeting creates a framework within which individuals, departments, and whole organizations can work. Budgets encourage individuals and departments to look and plan ahead using a standardized agenda that can enhance effective communication of their objectives. Drafting assorted budgets and collating them can help co-ordinate and motivate employees. Budgets also provide a focus for evaluation of the various aspects of a business in a controlled fashion.

THE SIX MAIN AIMS OF BUDGETING

AIMS	DESCRIPTION
PLANNING	To aid the planning of an organization in a systematic and logical manner that adheres to the long-term business strategy.
CO-ORDINATION	To help co-ordinate the activities of the various parts of the organization and ensure that they are consistent.
COMMUNICATION	To communicate more easily the objectives, opportunities, and plans of the business to the various business team managers.
MOTIVATION	To provide motivation for managers to try to achieve the organizational and individual goals.
CONTROL	To help control activities by measuring progress against the original plan, adjusting where necessary.
EVALUATION	To provide a framework for evaluating the performance of managers in meeting individual and departmental targets.

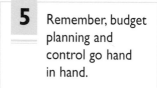

5 Remember, budget planning and control go hand in hand.

6 Plan what you are going to do, do not just react to changes.

EVALUATING THE DISADVANTAGES

A conscientious and effective budget brings numerous benefits to an organization, yet a budget can be inconvenient. Assess the disadvantages of preparing a budget in the light of its many advantages.

- Budgets increase paperwork and can be a drain on management time, especially early on.
- Budgets are slow to work, since the benefits will not be seen until the next year.
- Budgets require standardization, which can lead to inflexibility.
- Budgets can meet with resistance from managers reluctant to embrace new procedures.

BUDGETING AND BUSINESS STRATEGY

The budgeting process is a relatively short-term measure that is just one part of the overall business strategy. It is a tactic that is used in the implementation of activities and programs for which senior management will have planned.

> **7** Tell your money where to go; do not worry about where it went.

> **8** Make sure your organization has clearly thought out long-term plans and strategies.

UNDERSTANDING BUSINESS STRATEGY

Business strategy is the vision of where the organization wants to be in three to five years' time. This will include setting overall objectives so that the organization can determine what it hopes to achieve. The business strategy also identifies courses of action. This involves analyzing the environment in which an organization operates and the resources that it possesses using the SWOT analysis – an assessment of the business strengths, weaknesses, opportunities, and threats.

DEVELOPING THE BUSINESS PLAN

Whereas organizations plan for the long term using a strategic plan, they plan for the short-term using a business plan – what the organization must do now in order to achieve the strategic plan. In order to put into practice the business plan, the organization must consider appropriate planning procedures to work out what to do when, and the necessary controls (including budgeting) to ensure that anticipated results are actually achieved.

THINGS TO DO

1. Inspect the strategic plan.
2. Review the SWOT analysis.
3. Examine other business assessments.
4. Inspect the business plan.
5. Understand the context of your budget within the overall business.

USING A BUDGET AS A BUSINESS TACTIC

Budgeting is the tactical implementation of the business plan. It is incorporated in both the business planning and control processes. Senior management choose the strategic options that will have the greatest potential for achieving the organization's objectives and will create long-term plans to implement those strategies. You can transform those long-range plans into your department's budgeted annual operating plans. Use budgets as a benchmark against which you can measure actual future performance by using regular internally-generated financial reports called the management accounting package. This package is made up from the profit-and-loss accounts, balance sheets, and cash flow financial reports, and shows what was expected compared to what actually happened.

9 Consider the market trends of your organization's products.

10 Use budgets to judge performance and as an authority to spend.

THE BUSINESS PLANNING AND CONTROL PROCESS

STAGE	ACTIONS TO TAKE
SHORT-TERM PLANNING	● Prepare operating plans and programs. ● Compile annual financial budgets. ● React to changes in the marketplace. ● Continually reassess validity of plans.
LONG-TERM PLANNING	● Determine the organization's business objectives. ● Evaluate strategic market and product options. ● Analyze the organization's strengths and weaknesses. ● Identify financial, physical, and human resource needs.
CONTROL	● Prepare management reports. ● Evaluate discrepancies between actual and plan. ● Decide on how to remedy discrepancies. ● Take effective corrective action.

MAINTAINING A BUSINESS BUDGETING CYCLE

There is a popular misconception that the annual budgeting event is a ballistic process: you do a lot of work, then you press a button and you're off. Everything is then put away until next year. In fact, quite the opposite is true. Far from being a discrete once-a-year activity, budgeting requires continuous and simultaneous tending of budgeted and actual figures from several accounting years. In every month in the year, there will be a budgeting-related activity taking place in an organization. This activity could be for one of several years – the year just gone, the current year, the year to come, or several years to come. This activity could also be of several types – budget preparation, budget monitoring, updating estimates, finalizing whole year results, or looking ahead longer-term.

 11 Ensure that your budgeting is a year-round continuous process.

12 Schedule your budgeting-related tasks in financially less busy periods.

POINTS TO REMEMBER

● Budgeting activity may be for this year, next year, or several years into the future.

● Budgeting activities repeat themselves, usually over the course of a year, and should therefore be anticipated.

● Realistic planning will help you to carry out budgeting-related tasks in a logical order.

 13 Allow sufficient time in your budgeting schedule to do justice to your budgeting process.

CULTURAL DIFFERENCES

Most European countries regard budgeting as a necessary management tool without which an organization cannot survive. However, the US and certain Scandinavian countries are increasingly seeing budgeting as a tool of repression that does little to improve business health. These countries see little value in continuing to work to figures from a budget that bear little resemblance to the actual figures that are produced from the changing real world. Many of the techniques used in these countries as an alternative to traditional budgeting follow a more holistic approach. An example is the balanced business scorecard technique, which considers all aspects of a business rather than just its financial concerns.

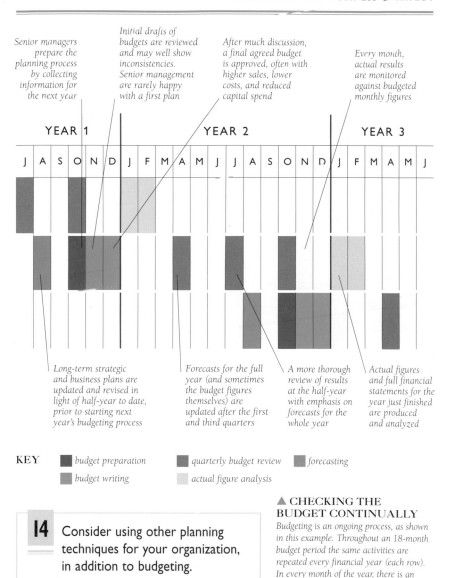

Senior managers prepare the planning process by collecting information for the next year

Initial drafts of budgets are reviewed and may well show inconsistencies. Senior management are rarely happy with a first plan

After much discussion, a final agreed budget is approved, often with higher sales, lower costs, and reduced capital spend

Every month, actual results are monitored against budgeted monthly figures

YEAR 1	YEAR 2	YEAR 3
J A S O N D	J F M A M J J A S O N D	J F M A M J

Long-term strategic and business plans are updated and revised in light of half-year to date, prior to starting next year's budgeting process

Forecasts for the full year (and sometimes the budget figures themselves) are updated after the first and third quarters

A more thorough review of results at the half-year with emphasis on forecasts for the whole year

Actual figures and full financial statements for the year just finished are produced and analyzed

KEY
- budget preparation
- quarterly budget review
- forecasting
- budget writing
- actual figure analysis

14 Consider using other planning techniques for your organization, in addition to budgeting.

▲ CHECKING THE BUDGET CONTINUALLY

Budgeting is an ongoing process, as shown in this example. Throughout an 18-month budget period the same activities are repeated every financial year (each row). In every month of the year, there is an aspect of budgeting that requires attention.

MANAGING THE BUDGETING PROCESS

Just as budgeting is part of the structured business model of planning and control, so is there a structured model for managing the budgeting process itself. It is important to use a model as a blueprint for the process to ensure consistency and quality.

15 Ensure that you know what you intend to do at every stage.

16 Always plan, even if the future is unpredictable.

17 Co-ordinate your budget with other departments.

TAILORING THE MODEL

Budgeting is too important to get wrong, and a manager will often not get a second chance. Within reason, make your budgets as accurate as possible on the first attempt. Following a model will help you to get it right the first time. It will not guarantee success, but the quality of what is produced will be greatly improved. As with all models, tailor your budgeting process to suit your departmental needs in tune with your business environment. If something in the model is not relevant to your organization, do not do it.

COPING WITH AN UNCERTAIN FUTURE

The future is uncertain, so what is the point of trying to predict it accurately? Many will claim that the uncertainties specific to their business make budgets impractical for them, yet one can always find companies in the same industry that use budgets successfully. Even in fast-moving sectors, such as information technology and telecommunications, you will find that many of the companies that regard budgets as indispensable are among the industry leaders. As a manager, it is important that you grapple with any uncertainties early on, and that you are prepared to be flexible in your approach to budgeting. Always bear in mind that the benefits of good budgeting will always exceed the cost.

FOLLOWING THE BUDGETING MODEL

PREPARING	WRITING	MONITORING

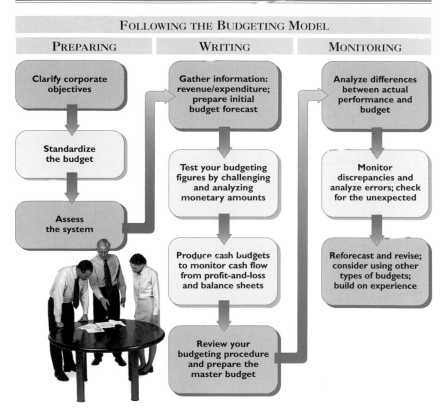

Clarify corporate objectives

Standardize the budget

Assess the system

Gather information: revenue/expenditure; prepare initial budget forecast

Test your budgeting figures by challenging and analyzing monetary amounts

Produce cash budgets to monitor cash flow from profit-and-loss and balance sheets

Review your budgeting procedure and prepare the master budget

Analyze differences between actual performance and budget

Monitor discrepancies and analyze errors; check for the unexpected

Reforecast and revise; consider using other types of budgets; build on experience

FOLLOWING A STRUCTURE

Build three distinct, but equally important, tasks into your budgeting model. First, you should prepare the budget; second, you should write the budget; finally you must monitor the budget. Research has shown that most budgets that fail to achieve their purpose have been neither properly planned nor properly monitored. Organizations often jump straight into writing a budget, without any thought or preparation, and have nothing to refer to later on in the budgeting cycle.

THINGS TO DO

1. Plan your budgeting model.
2. Decide on the personnel that you want involved.
3. Communicate the plan to key people.
4. Allocate sufficient budget resources.

Tailors approach to organizational needs

Supports organizational objectives

Standardizes certain procedures

Ensures personal flexibility

Follows simple rules

BEGINNING TO BUDGET ▲

There are a number of qualities that a manager must possess in order to manage budgeting effectively. If any one of these qualities is absent, your budgeting efficiency will soon be reduced.

---

18 Write out the important tasks on a calendar to help with the timing of key steps within your budget.

PREPARING TO BUDGET

The importance of "planning the plan" can not be over-emphasized, and you must understand how a budget can be made to work for your organization. Rather than expecting someone else's budgeting model to work for you, you must tailor your budget to your organization. A superb document is worthless if it does not comply with your organization's strategic plan. Preparing to budget also involves standardizing procedures. It can be useful to create a budgeting manual that provides budgeting guidelines which, depending on the size of your organization, can be monitored by a committee.

DO'S AND DON'TS

✔ Do encourage your team to plan ahead to reduce the number of ad hoc decisions.

✔ Do communicate management plans and listen to the problems that others foresee.

✔ Do provide a yardstick against which other managers and their departments' performances can be evaluated.

✘ Don't expect to reconcile and merge separate functional budgets without any co-ordination.

✘ Don't accept anything other than reasonable, well-defined targets to encourage motivation.

✘ Don't forget to allocate resources appropriately and openly for managers and departments.

---

19 Consider using project-planning software for more complex budgets.

---

20 Ask friends in other departments to show you how they budget.

WRITING A BUDGET ▼
If all managers follow the same standard procedures for writing budgets, senior management will be able to evaluate all budgets in relation to each other, for the good of the whole organization.

Chairperson evaluates the requirements of all departments

Manager reports on own department

WRITING A BUDGET

There are a number of logical steps to writing a meaningful budget. Initially, you must gather information about what your organization wants to achieve, what its limits are, and what the relevant internal and external business influences are that will affect the organization. It is crucial that you focus on the types, amounts, and timings of both revenue and costs to give you better estimates for income and expenditure. To be more efficient, provide more valid figures, and know how to challenge budgeted amounts you must understand cost types and behavior. Linking the capital expenditure budgets to revenue and expenditure will give senior management a clearer picture of the feasibility of a budget, and you must carry out an all-important consolidation process to finalize the budget.

MONITORING A BUDGET

It is vital that you monitor a budget by checking what actually happened against what you budgeted to happen, investigating the reasons why there are discrepancies, taking corrective action, then assessing how you could improve your budgeting in the future. It is important to know what to do when the budget seems to be plainly wrong: whether it should be left alone or changed, and how changes should be made. Some of the inaccuracies in a budget may be due to human errors rather than business issues, so it is important to consider all the various factors before you begin to build for the future.

21 Tailor writing your budget to those aspects that you want to monitor.

22 See if there is a trend in the accuracy of previous budgets.

RECOGNIZING POTENTIAL PROBLEMS

In some organizations, budgets are regarded as something to be feared rather than as positive business tools that enhance performance. This is because budget systems serve several interests, some of which may conflict with each other.

23 Demanding but achievable targets are the most successful.

Managers meet to discuss and attempt to resolve conflicts

UNDERSTANDING CONFLICTS

By predicting potential conflicts of interest you will be able to set a realistic budget.

- Planning a demanding budget may lead to higher than realistically achievable figures, which can lead to demotivation among staff and poor performance.
- Business decisions that look good from an individual's perspective might prove to be less good for the department or whole organization.
- The business environment may be so fast-moving that the budget, as a tool or prediction, cannot keep up with events fast enough.

Conflicts remain unresolved and budget is likely to fail

DEALING WITH CONFLICTS

Budgeting is an imperfect science, and it is important to recognize that without corrective action conflicts can be become very disruptive.

- To motivate staff without compromising departmenal plans, produce two budgets: one for planning purposes and one for setting management targets.
- Give clear instructions to managers that they must act in accordance not only with their own interests but also those of the department.
- To ensure the budget is up to date, allow for a short budget timeframe, such as three months.

24 Communicate with others to avoid potential budgeting problems.

Managers understand each others' needs and agree how to keep to budget.

DISCUSSING ▲ WITH OTHERS
This illustration shows how by resolving potential conflicts early on, a budget can be successfully adhered to.

25 Organize training sessions that deal with budgeting best practice.

DO'S AND DON'TS

✔ Do recognize that budgets are used for more purposes than simply predicting next year's results.	✘ Don't confuse the organization's needs with what you want to achieve.
✔ Do accept that depending on the purpose and use of the figures, budgets can conflict.	✘ Don't get so drawn into interdepartmental politics that you begin to lose sight of the organization's aims.
✔ Do collaborate with other departmental managers to reach agreement.	✘ Don't keep to a budget that is clearly out of step with a fast-moving business; revise the budget.

PREPARING TO BUDGET

The better prepared your budget, the fewer problems you will have in the future. Link your budget to the objectives of your organization and provide a procedure that all can follow.

TAILORING A BUDGET

Your ultimate goal should be to create a budgeting system that actively supports the success of your organization. To achieve this you must prepare a budget that is tailored to your department and that fits in with the ambitions of your organization.

26 Learn from those who have done their budgets well in the past.

27 Take care not to be overambitious; it is a common error in a first budget submission.

WHY TAILOR THE BUDGET?

It is very important early on that you determine how you are going set out your own budgeting style. Budgeting can fulfill a number of functions. It can be a means by which to help achieve business targets, measure business performance, appraise managers and departments, and motivate staff. Consider which functions are most important to your department and organization and build your budgeting style and reporting around them. Remember that the budgeting process is a means to an end, not the end in itself.

DEVISING A RELEVANT BUDGET

Make sure that you do not devise a rigid and unyielding budget in which everything is categorized as a success or failure. You will not set a useful budget if you set unrealistic targets and try to measure performance against them. Approach budgeting in a pragmatic manner so that it is effective as a business tool and not an impediment to your success. Do not be tempted to slavishly follow someone else's budget model. Set the headings yourself based on your own assessment of your needs. Keep in mind that budgeting priorities can change and that you may need to adapt your budget to serve a constantly changing business environment. It can be helpful early on to review those budgeting activities that have taken place within your organization in the past. How successful were they, what should be improved upon, and what should be added to make this year's budgeting even better? Finally, as a rule of thumb, bear in mind that it will take one or two years to set up a reliable system that can run effectively.

28 Avoid unnecessary jargon to help convey your budgeting aims.

THINGS TO DO

1. Publicize the fact that budgeting will take place.
2. Educate staff about what the budgeting process will do for the department.
3. Consider how accurate you want your first budgeting attempt to be.
4. Establish your department's goals for success and prepare a budget that reflects those aims.

BUDGETING FOR YOUR NEEDS

No two organizations are the same. Every organization will budget differently and should not blindly borrow practices from others. You need to decide why you are budgeting, what you want to achieve from it, what your particular business problems are, and how your approach to budgeting will meet these aims.

CASE STUDY

Felicity's Foods maintained food vending machines in corporate offices. The company had never really budgeted for any future activities before, but was anxious to do so as its sales were growing fast.

The accountant suggested a budgeting model that he used in his last job at Megahuge plc, a manufacturing company, which he said worked well.

However, senior managers were worried that the budget model would not be relevant for a business of their size.

The accountant resolved the problem by revising the budget model to include only those elements of the borrowed budget that were relevant to the size of Felicity's Foods' business, and he omitted any details that were inappropriate.

As a result, senior management were much happier, and agreed to use the tailored budgeting model as a pilot run for the following year.

CLARIFYING OBJECTIVES

Base your budget on a clear, objective organizational strategy. Determine this strategy early on by reviewing your departmental business to compare actual results with ideal results, then prepare a budgeting plan to close that gap.

29 Clarify objectives in a brainstorming session with other managers.

30 Be innovative with the financial ratios you choose.

THE FOUR STEPS ▼
Base budgets on a four step approach that will help you to clarify your department's business objectives in financial terms.

STEP 4
Set financial targets

STEP 3
Decide objectives

STEP 2
Plan for the future

STEP 1
Review the business

REVIEWING THE BUSINESS

You must carry out a thoroughly realistic and honest departmental review that looks at all parts of the business that affect its capacity to deliver what the customer wants. The review procedure gives you an opportunity to look at your department with an objective budgeting eye, which can be both an exhilarating and leveling process. The important thing is that it must be well-informed and honest. This is not the time for fault-finding or fantasy. The lessons of the past should only be viewed as a tool for acting effectively in the future. The popular SWOT analysis (strengths, weaknesses, opportunities and threats) is a good starting point for the review, though other structured and objective techniques can be just as effective.

DO'S AND DON'TS

✔ Do make sure that you fully appreciate the true strengths and opportunities that your department and organization possess.

✔ Do be fully aware of the enormous amount of time and effort that budgeting requires.

✘ Don't be afraid to recognize honestly the weaknesses and threats that your business faces.

✘ Don't copy business objectives from other departments, make sure you generate your own.

PLANNING FOR THE FUTURE

The strategic plan sets out the major long-term business and financial plans for your organization and is the basis on which you will set your department's objectives. The strategic plan could simply state the definition of your business and how your organization plans to grow in terms of size, quality, security, and competitiveness.

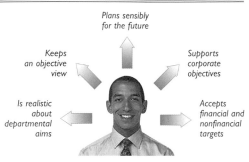

Plans sensibly for the future

Keeps an objective view

Supports corporate objectives

Is realistic about departmental aims

Accepts financial and nonfinancial targets

▲ FOLLOW BUSINESS OBJECTIVES

It is from the definition of the strategic plan that you will be able to set your all-important business objectives and link your organization's strategy to your department's operational control.

31 Avoid too many backward-looking measures.

32 In business, there is always something to be standardized.

DECIDING CORPORATE OBJECTIVES

Business objectives consider the business as a whole and may be only partly quantifiable. Some objectives are general; others relate specifically to marketing, organizational, or financial concerns. Setting objectives for your department allows you to define your aspirations in ways that can be used to measure the business. You will achieve much more by remembering to balance what is achievable with what is aspirational.

SETTING FINANCIAL TARGETS

Convert your department's objectives into a formal financial budget. This should take into account marketing, production (or provisions of services), purchasing, personnel, and administration. Express these financial targets in profit-and-loss accounts, balance sheets, and cash flow statements, year by year, for the whole budget period. To cover all aspects of your business, you should also include in your budget nonfinancial perfomance measures, such as recorded complaints and compliments.

CHOOSING THE BUDGET PERIOD

The budget period is the length of time the budget covers, usually one year. It is often sub-divided into control periods of varying lengths, usually monthly. Choose your budget period by defining the level of budgetary control you wish to exercise.

STANDARDIZING A BUDGET

To co-ordinate budgets within your
organization, managers should use
a standard budgeting format. This will help
with collaboration over budget content and
enable budgets to be compared and linked
throughout your organization.

33 Issue blank budgets as spreadsheets for electronic completion.

34 Publicize the purpose of the budget committee and its activities.

COMPILING A MANUAL

An effective budget manual needs to include
the following:

- An introduction to the importance of budgeting.
- A timetable showing when the master budget will be prepared from all other budgets.
- Guidelines to common key assumptions to be made by managers in their budgets.
- Copies of forms to be completed, including explanations concerning their completion.
- An organizational chart with names of those that are responsible for each budget.
- Departmental account codes and names of contacts to help with budgeting problems.

DEVISING A MANUAL ▼
*A budget manual need not be much more
than a few sheets of paper listing key facts
to make sure that everyone is working
with the same basic figures in mind.*

*Shows standard
assumptions
about external
matters affecting
the budget
preparation*

*Gives the
organization's
estimate for likely
prices and market
conditions*

*Shows nontrading
items, such as tax,
exchange, interest,
and inflation rates*

EXTERNAL MATTERS
1. The market is not expected to grow by
much more than 20% per a
each of the next 5 years. Ou
is that 10% is likely to be th
growth rate in sales that wo
achieve.
2. Markets are currently pric
and our economic forecast
no early end to this trend.
zero price increase next y
3. Interest rates of 6.5% are
for all calculations.
4. For those with foreign eu
exposure in Europe assu
For other currency rates
contact Treasury depart
5. Assume 2.5% inflation a
board.
6. Tax rates will remain u
throughout the year.

INTERNAL MATTERS
1. Headcount is to maintained at current
levels and wage increases will be limited
to 3% at all levels.
2. The timetable below highlights key
milestone dates in the budget - please
be aware of them.
3. This year certain departments are being
asked to prepare budgets on a different
basis - see zero based budgeting.
4. Below is an organization chart showing
how your budget fits in, and who to go
to for help.

5. We aim to pay all suppliers within 60
days and collect monies from customers
in the same time.

*Gives details of
estimates about
internal matters
affecting the budget*

*Presents structural
matters, such as
changes to
employee numbers
and likely wage
settlements*

*Provides consistent
benchmarks for
dealing with
customers and
suppliers*

Q How could we possibly improve on the effectiveness of last year's budget?

Q Are all managers in the budgeting process familiar with the standardized procedures?

Q How far in advance of the budgeting process should the manual be issued?

Q What is the minimum number of people I need on the budgeting committee?

Q Does the budgeting committee have the right mix of skills, seniority, and relevant people?

FORMING A COMMMITTEE

A budget cannot be prepared without reference to other departmental budgets, and so some degree of budgetary co-ordination is required. By forming a budget committee that includes representatives from the various business departments, you will be able to monitor the departmental budgeting progress and resolve any problems that might arise. The budgeting committee should set the guidelines for the budgeting manual, review departmental budgets by studying budget forecasts at meetings, create a master budget, be a general budgeting trouble-shooter, and ensure that the whole process is completed effectively and on time.

COMMITTEE MEMBERS ▼
A budgeting committee should comprise senior managers from the major business segments, the management accountant, and heads of all departments involved in the budget preparations.

35 Arrange for the budget committee to meet regularly.

Accountant is committee's technical advisor

Chairperson controls and mediates

Manager represents his department

CREATING A FORM

A budget form is the standardized actual layout that is used to collect and display all the information that goes into a budget. While most organizations should insist on standard forms (especially for the key areas of income, costs, and capital), some do allow a degree of flexibility appropriate to specific individual circumstances. Keep five principles in mind to ensure that the form looks good, is easy to use, and is efficient:

● Keep the form simple and straightforward, with only necessary details.
● Avoid amateur and overenthusiastic artwork.
● All forms should be consistent, with similar layout, typeface, and design.
● The form should be logically presented, well-organized, and be understandable without instructions.
● Wherever possible, use spreadsheets or the equivalent to ensure easy capture of data and ease of subsequent processing.

▼ USING FORMS
Everyone involved in filling in a budget form will do things differently. To end up with figures that are homogenous and can be easily added together, you must design a form that can be used by everyone.

A well-presented, standard form is easy for everyone to use

Notes on specific details can be taken and referred to at a later date

---

QUESTIONS TO ASK YOURSELF

Q Is the form good enough to stand on its own?

Q Are its contents clear and easy to understand?

Q Does it answer all likely questions?

Q Will the budget committee need more details?

Q Has it been fully completed in all significant respects?

Q Will other managers be able to fill in similar forms?

COMPLETING A FORM

When filling in a form, always keep one question in mind: "Am I completing the form correctly?" Ensure that you have inserted figures accurately and they have been added or subtracted correctly. Check that information is correctly arranged in columns and rows and that decimal points and commas are in the right places. Try to make the form as intelligible as possible. Correct all grammar, spelling, and punctuation; avoid using jargon, slang, technical or vague expressions; and keep words and phrases short. Give the form to someone else, perhaps another manager, to check that they can understand its content.

CENTURY COPIERS FORM TR1/99

TRADING RESULTS	YEAR DATE												
	Jan	Feb	Mar	Apr	May	Jun	Jul	Aug	Sep	Oct	Nov	Dec	TOTAL
TURNOVER	940	1,100	1,200	960	980	1,150	1,060	850	1,200	1,250	1,500	1,310	13,500
COST OF SALES	705	840	910	740	730	880	820	650	910	950	1,100	980	10,215
GROSS PROFIT	235	260	290	220	250	270	240	200	290	300	400	330	3,285
GROSS PROFIT MARGIN	25%	24%	24%	23%	26%	23%	23%	24%	24%	24%	27%	25%	24%
OVERHEADS:													
Salaries	56	57	57	54	60	62	55	58	56	55	52	53	675
Pensions	6	6	6	6	6	6	6	6	5	5	5	5	68
Motor and travel	6	7	7	7	7	7	6	6	7	7	7	7	81
Equipment rental	1	1	1	1	1	1	1	1	1	1	1	1	12
Telecom	10	9	11	11	10	10	11	10	9	10	10	11	122
Print, post & stationery	4	4	5	5	5	6	4	4	4	5	4	4	54
Marketing	10	11	11	12	12	11	13	12	11	11	11	10	135
Storage	3	3	3	4	3	3	3	4	3	4	4	4	41
Maintenance	12	12	11	12	13	12	12	11	12	13	13	13	149
Heat, light & power	20	20	20	22	20	19	19	18	19	22	21	23	243
Insurance	8	8	8	7	9	9	9	10	8	8	8	9	101
Rent and rates	34	34	34	34	34	34	34	34	34	34	33	32	405
Legal & professional	1	1	1	1	3	1	1	1	1	2	1	2	16
Sundries	3	3	3	3	4	4	4	4	4	4	4	5	45
Depreciation	22	22	22	20	21	21	21	23	25	24	24	25	270
Bad debts	2	2	3	4	2	2	3	2	3	3	4	4	34
Profit on sale of assets	1	1	1		1	1	1	3	1	1	1	2	14
TOTAL OVERHEADS	199	201	204	203	211	209	203	210	203	209	203	210	2,465
OPERATING PROFIT (LOSS)	36	59	86	17	39	61	37	-10	87	91	197	120	820
Interest payable	5	5	5	5	5	5	5	5	5	5	5	5	60
NET PROFIT	31	54	81	12	34	56	32	-15	82	86	192	115	760

Reference code/number that can be quoted in later discussions

Clearly-defined columns and rows help to structure information

Black figures on a white background are easy to refer to for subsequent processing

Key calculations are segregated for easy reference

List of essential revenue and expenditure headings, ordered in a logical and progressive way

36 Use only listed options in spreadsheet cells to ensure there is consistency.

▲ **DEVISING THE LAYOUT**
Time spent on a well-created form is never wasted. Not only will it portray a well-presented and professional image, it can be understood easily by colleagues, and, importantly, can be easily referred to during later budget discussions.

REVIEWING YOUR SYSTEM

Once all the preparations for the budget have been made, you are ready to begin writing the budget and drafting the figures. Before you do that, review your system to ensure that your budget will provide you with correct and relevant information.

37 Deliberately putting padding into budgets achieves nothing.

38 Responsibility and accountability must go together.

39 Ensure you check the budget with the right people.

KEEPING TO YOUR PLAN

Try not to dive straight into the budget. Remember the pareto rule: you can get 80 per cent of the result with only 20 per cent of the effort, but without proper planning the remaining 20 per cent of the result can take up to 80 per cent of the effort. Achieve successful preparation by ensuring that you have personalized and tailored your approach, linked the budget to organizational objectives, and used a few standardized procedures. Much of this is simply common sense and good practice, but it is often ignored in the rush to produce figures.

FOLLOWING THE GOLDEN RULES

While budgets should be flexible and tailored to suit individual and departmental circumstances, you must also double-check that your budget is compatible with others and that there is a degree of standardization throughout the organization. You can achieve this not only through the use of budget manuals and forms but also by ensuring that everyone involved in the budgeting process keeps to the same principles of budget preparation. Keep following a list of rules for the whole budgeting process to ensure greater consistency and to realize the budget's full potential.

POINTS TO REMEMBER

- Use your colleagues' expertise and knowledge in the business review and planning process.
- Challenge present limits to your business and be inventive about how these could be overcome.
- Widen the organization's measurement perspective to beyond purely financial matters and include other significant objectives.
- Be pragmatic: a budget is a practical tool so it must be realistic and easy to use.

EIGHT GOLDEN RULES FOR EFFECTIVE BUDGETS

GOLDEN RULES	PUTTING THEORY INTO PRACTICE
BUDGET CONTINUOUSLY Budgeting and planning are not just one-time events.	Consider budgeting as more than an annual activity. Remember that the future is uncertain, so revise budgets regularly to reflect changes in the business environment.
TAKE YOUR TIME Budgets are the key part of planning and require careful thinking.	Do not underestimate the time needed to gather relevant information, formulate plans, and make a budget a realistic planning proposal.
INVOLVE EVERYONE Include all those that should be involved in the budgeting process.	Make your budgeting more than just a high-level activity. Involve relevant people with appropriate knowledge and skills and encourage them to commit to the process.
BE REALISTIC Focus on what your deparment actually needs in a particular budget.	Be aware that if resources are scarce there will be competing demands for items within the organization, which can often lead to deliberate overestimation.
LOOK AHEAD Look to the future, not to the past when deciding budgeting amounts.	Keep focused on future targets. Do not rely on historic figures to guide next year's budget, which, although approximately right, might be completely wrong.
BE AWARE OF POLITICS The size of budget does not equal its importance in the organization.	Understand that the size of a budget should not be confused with importance, and avoid all traditional budgetary game-playing around this.
MONITOR EVENTS Priorities and amounts may need to be changed in line with events.	Be prepared to amend your budget while still challenging all expenditures and trying to resolve unforeseen problems in other ways.
ALLOW FLEXIBILITY Budgets do not have to be slavishly followed.	Avoid the temptation to spend all that you were authorized to, and do not guard an underspend in your budget when others could well use the resource.

WRITING A BUDGET

To write a budget you must gather information, estimate figures for income and expenditure, and bring everything together in one agreed overall document.

GATHERING INFORMATION

*B*y gathering information on all the possible internal and external influences on your budget, you will be able to determine what can and what cannot be achieved and what limiting factors might constrain your organization's activities.

> **40** Be aware of changing business laws and requirements.

CULTURAL DIFFERENCES

Government legislation in different countries can make the business environment liberal or authoritarian, and employment costs can affect labor mobility and the availability of skills. There are also different cross-cultural attitudes to payments from customers and to suppliers.

ASSESSING EXTERNAL INFLUENCES

External influences can have a greater effect on the success of a business than internal influences, so pay them close attention. Many organizations fail because they simply do not take the time to understand what is happening and what is about to happen around them. The main external influences that can affect your budget can be grouped into three areas: economic, population, and labor matters; governments and statutory bodies; and the business relationship between customers and suppliers.

POSSIBLE EXTERNAL INFLUENCES ON A BUDGET

AREA OF INFLUENCE	FACTORS TO CONSIDER
ECONOMIC, POPULATION, AND LABOR	**ECONOMY** Structure, cycle, inflation rates, interest rates, taxation levels, world influence, stock markets.
	POPULATION Types, number, location, mobility, births, deaths, future trends.
	COMMUNITY Neighbors, pressure groups, environmental issues, local differences, social trends, cultural trends.
	LABOR Types, number, availability, response to training, demands, expectations, skill sets.
GOVERNMENTS AND STATUTORY BODIES	**LEGISLATION** Employment law, consumer protection, health and safety, competition laws, statutory bodies.
	GOVERNMENT Types, fiscal and monetary policy, industrial and competition policy, incentives and initiatives.
	INTERNATIONAL TRADE AGREEMENTS Exports and imports, trade tariffs, tax harmonization, trade quotas, exchange rates.
	ORGANIZATIONS IRS, state tax bodies, creditors, lenders, stakeholders, management, regulatory bodies.
BUSINESS RELATIONSHIP BETWEEN CUSTOMERS AND SUPPLIERS	**CUSTOMERS** Types and numbers, demand levels, financial viability, likely growth, wants and needs.
	COMPETITORS Location, products, activities, strengths and weaknesses, attrition rate, aggression, growth rates.
	SUPPLIERS Types and numbers, cost and levels of supply, partnership, reliance, financial viability, location.

ASSESSING INTERNAL INFLUENCES

Assessing the influence that internal factors will have on a budget may seem simple enough but, because the focus is now inward-looking, sometimes obvious matters can be overlooked. There are three main areas of influence: business influences such as products and services; higher-level factors such as directors or shareholders; and resource availability. Since checklists cannot be exhaustive, always consider what other factors might apply; from the volatility of the business, through restructuring or change initiatives, to quality of management.

 41 Recognize the importance of good management.

POINTS TO REMEMBER

- Internal factors may change and should be assessed continuously.
- Internal discussions can be the best source of information.
- Significant events should be anticipated.

POSSIBLE INTERNAL INFLUENCES ON A BUDGET

AREA OF INFLUENCE	FACTORS TO CONSIDER
BUSINESS INFLUENCES	**PRODUCTS AND SERVICES** Types, number, production methods, prices, pricing methods, stock levels
	BUSINESS UNITS Sales, production, purchasing, marketing, finance, administration, personnel
HIGH-LEVEL FACTORS	**PEOPLE** Directors, shareholders, unions, employees
	BUSINESS OBJECTIVES Short term, medium term, long term
RESOURCE AVAILABILITY	**AVAILABLE RESOURCES** Capital, profits, land, buildings, plant and equipment, machinery
	DEPARTMENTAL BUDGETS Sales, production, purchasing, marketing, finance, administration, personnel

ASSESSING THE LIMITING FACTOR

A limiting factor is a dominating influence that has a constraining effect on your department and organization. Although it may seem theoretical, the concept is only too real for most businesses. Identify limiting factors early in the budgeting process because they will determine the order in which you prepare individual budgets. If you fail to recognize a limiting factor you may set yourself targets that are just not achievable. There will probably be only one limiting factor; usually it is sales or the capacity to produce, though sometimes the marketplace may be the limit, especially if it is monopolistic and anticompetitive, stagnant, or subject to quotas. Other limiting factors include shortages or irregularities in raw materials, labor investment and machinery, or there might be physical constraints on property and premises.

QUESTIONS TO ASK YOURSELF

Q Does the organization's constitution allow us to perform planned activities?

Q Is planning permission for expansion likely to be granted?

Q Do we have access to enough capital to achieve our plan?

Q Are we in a small marketplace with a limited customer base?

Q Can we attract people with sufficient skills to our location?

42 Be aware that it is not always sales that limit an organization.

43 Be honest and objective with your assessment of internal influences.

44 Keep informed by reading your internal business communications.

LIMITING FACTOR REMEDIES

What can be done to stop something being a limiting factor? Constraints can be temporary, so recognize that a limiting factor can change from year to year.

● If the limiting factor is sales, consider cutting the price of goods and services, and increase the media advertising budget.

● To remove capacity constraints, spend more on plant and machinery or contemplate outsourcing production.

● If labor is scarce, either pay more or recruit from other, non-traditional, labor pools.

ANTICIPATING REVENUES

Most budgets are driven by the overall level of sales, so to produce an accurate budget you must correctly estimate the type, amount, and timing of revenues. Focus on the sources of income, their likely volume and price, and the timing of receipts.

45 Customers usually take twice as long to pay than you would expect.

ASSESSING REVENUE TYPES

Estimating overall sales revenues is likely to be the hardest task in the budgeting process, since you can only guess what the future holds. However, if you divide revenues – which will be almost entirely sales of goods and services – into subheadings, such as types of product, market segment, and geographical location you can at least make your estimates easier to access. The purpose is to make subsequent analysis, discussion, and monitoring of revenues easier to undertake; so organize your revenue types into sufficient detail without being excessive.

Manager explains why his sales figures underachieved last year

New products to achieve increased sales next year

DO'S AND DON'TS

✔ Do liase with other departments to anticipate next year's new revenue streams.

✔ Do be realistic about how far to subdivide income types for analysis purposes.

✘ Don't be constrained by looking only at the revenue types that arose last year.

✘ Don't restrict analysis to ongoing revenues; consider capital and one-time events.

▲ **ESTIMATING REVENUES**
Analyze recent history, anticipate the future, and liaise closely with other departments to ensure an accurate budget.

46 Estimate the likely price elasticity of demand for sales.

ESTIMATING REVENUE AMOUNTS

Arriving at a realistic figure for sales revenue owes much to inspired guesswork and luck. Typically, figures will be based on what happened in the previous year, since this approach is based on some reality. It is important to get an estimate of what really could be achieved with commitment and effort, rather than through minor marginal improvements. Ask the sales department to build up figures based on customer histories, current developments, and local intelligence. Management's instinct, albeit subjective, is also a valid tool.

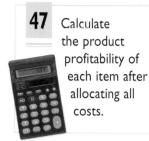

47 Calculate the product profitability of each item after allocating all costs.

▼ **PREDICTING INCOME**
To obtain an accurate prediction of income, focus on the three steps of income assessment.

| Types | Amounts | Timing |

48 Always keep an open mind when you look into the future.

PROJECTING REVENUE TIMING

The single most important control that you should exert within your department is monitoring cash flow. Most organizations can trade profitably, but run out of cash – the life-blood of a business. Typically, expenditure is paid before revenues are received, especially during times of growth, so it is essential that you control your cash timings. Be realistic, and even a little pessimistic, since most customers do not pay within their agreed terms. Talk to the accounting department about historical payment trends, and talk to the sales department about individual customers' current financial health and their likely future payment positions.

◀ **ANALYZING TIMING TRENDS**
Generally, sales revenue arrives later than expected. Look at payment trends and anticipate how these might change in the future, both overall and on an individual customer basis.

ESTIMATING EXPENDITURE

Actual expenditure is usually greater than that budgeted for. Organizations are often surprised by this, even though it happens every year. To ensure an accurate expenditure forecast, focus on the types, amounts, and timing of expenditure.

49 Remind yourself that not everything in a budget has to be spent.

ESTIMATING COSTS ▲
By understanding which of the four types of expenditure your costs are, you can assess how easy they will be to control.

ASSESSING EXPENDITURE TYPES

There are four main types of expenditure. Ongoing specific costs (costs driven by particular products and services) and ongoing shared costs (shared costs incurred for the whole organization) will be incurred by most organizations all the time on a routine basis. These are true annual recurring expenditure items, which should be relatively easy to estimate and control. Startup costs (incurred when starting or growing a new operation) and capital (or nonrevenue) costs are one-time items. They are usually harder to estimate because they do not happen often, and when they do the costs are likely to be different each time.

ESTIMATING THE AMOUNT OF EXPENDITURE

Expenditure must be estimated in terms of both quantities used and prices paid. There is no doubt that a list of possible activities and costs may appear limitless. Ask every relevant department and colleague about the probable quantities needed, prices payable, and total amounts for all the different possible costs. Although all the estimates will largely be based on previous experiences in similar circumstances, your intuition will play a significant part.

50 Check the previous year's expenditure to prevent omitting costs from this year's budget.

PROJECTING EXPENDITURE TIMING

Timing of expenditure is crucial to producing an accurate cashflow forecast, especially the timing of the largest expenditure. It is important to liaise with the purchasing department since they might have recently negotiated some expenditure timings; for example, they may have traded supplier prices with the timing of supplier invoices. Often, payments are made quarterly rather than monthly, and while some expenses are payable in advance, others are paid in arrears. Do not forget that there are significant infrequent (rather than one-time) costs, the most important one being taxation on profits.

51 Allow for the impact of inflation on anticipated expenditure.

52 Be aware that technological changes will affect your costs.

TYPES OF EXPENDITURE

TYPE	EXAMPLES
ONGOING SPECIFIC COSTS	Raw material and component parts, purchased services, goods for resale, labour and wages, after-sales support and service.
ONGOING SHARED COSTS	Rent, rates, utilities, insurance, repairs, infrastructure, finance charges, postage, stationery, advertising, telephone, transportation, and professional fees.
ONE-TIME STARTUP COSTS	Drawings, pre-trading items, setup costs, specifications, production lines, sales and marketing literature, and employment and retraining costs.
ONE-TIME CAPITAL NON-REVENUE COSTS	Tangible assets such as buildings, plant and equipment, office machinery, fixtures, fittings, motor cars, and intangible assets such as goodwill, brands, and intellectual property.

UNDERSTANDING COSTS

It is important to fully understand costs so that you can produce a more accurate budget that contains better predictions and provides a better basis for analysis and decisions. View costs from two perspectives: fixed or variable, and direct or indirect.

53 Remember, a fixed cost is a cost that remains even if an activity is not done.

POINTS TO REMEMBER

- Your budgeted fixed and variable costs must be checked to ensure they make financial sense – before your accountant sees them.
- Costs are often neither clearly fixed nor variable, but a combination of the two.
- Indirect (or shared) costs should be used in assessing the true profitability of products.
- Cost terminology can be disconcerting, but should be overcome.

STUDYING COST BEHAVIOR

You should understand what drives costs, so as to be clear on cause-and-effect (have you spent more because you are busier, or just less efficient?), to gain more accurate expenditure estimates, and to get more useful analysis. If an organization doubles its sales, will all, some, or none of its costs also double? Will raw material purchases double? They probably will. But will head office costs double? Almost certainly they will not. Why are certain costs incurred; is it for one, or for many purposes? How should the cost then be allocated between the goods, services, and departments that use the cost?

UNDERSTANDING FIXED AND VARIABLE COSTS

Judge cost behavior in terms of the way that the cost is linked to your organization's volume of activity, usually sales. Costs that stay the same when volume increases (or decreases) are fixed costs, for example, finance, personnel, head office building, administration. Costs that increase in proportion to volume are variable costs, for example, goods for resale, productive labor, raw materials, distribution. Stepped fixed costs are those costs that are fixed until capacity is reached, when another fixed cost is added.

54 Understanding cost behavior is fundamental.

55 Challenge any increases in shared costs.

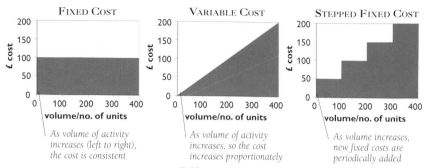

FIXED COST

As volume of activity increases (left to right), the cost is consistent

VARIABLE COST

As volume of activity increases, so the cost increases proportionally

STEPPED FIXED COST

As volume increases, new fixed costs are periodically added

DEFINING COSTS ▲
Other than for fixed costs, where cost is consistent, the price of costs changes as volume of activity increases.

56 Always try to get to the bottom of what drives indirect costs.

UNDERSTANDING DIRECT AND INDIRECT COSTS

A direct cost is incurred for the benefit of just one product or service, whereas an indirect cost is incurred for the benefit of many. Indirect costs are therefore sometimes known as shared costs. You must understand how to allocate indirect costs back to products and services. For example, you will need to decide how much of the head-office cost each item will bear. This will affect each product's profitability and can be used by senior management to assess its financial viability.

DIRECT AND INDIRECT COSTS

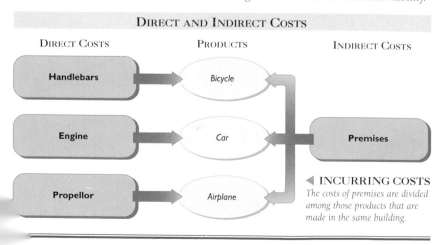

DIRECT COSTS

PRODUCTS

INDIRECT COSTS

Handlebars → Bicycle

Engine → Car ← Premises

Propellor → Airplane

◀ **INCURRING COSTS**
The costs of premises are divided among those products that are made in the same building.

PRODUCING THE FIGURES

Challenge the monetary amounts in your budget by testing the validity of your figures. Do this early on since initial budget submissions are rarely right, often sales figures will be optimistic and expenditure figures pessimistic.

57 Understand costs more clearly by showing them as a percentage of sales.

CHALLENGING MONETARY AMOUNTS

58 Remember, costs are driven by what must be achieved.

59 Check whether last year's figures are obviously wrong.

You should check and double-check your figures carefully. When the budget committee examines your first budgeting attempt you must be confident that you have submitted accurate figures. Budget committees are usually aware that experienced managers often build budgetary slack into their first submissions in anticipation of them being trimmed. In recognition of this common occurrence, you must allow for the budgeting committee simply to reduce your first budget submission by 10 percent.

USING THE OUTPUT/ INPUT METHOD

The Output/Input method is how you should approach producing the figures for your budget. Assess what your department produces (output), and ask yourself how this can be done, and then decide what resources are required to achieve this (input). It is all too easy to get this sequence the wrong way around. Avoid starting by assessing what resources you have and then trying to assess what can be achieved for the department. Categorize resources, people, and budgeted expenditure as inputs. Things that are made, work done, and services provided are outputs.

POINTS TO REMEMBER

● Inputs are determined by outputs, not the other way around.

● The required outputs, targets, and timings of the organization must be clarified.

● Alternative and challenging ideas can be generated in brainstorming sessions.

● The cost of required resources should be quantified financially.

● The quality and quantity of resources should be identified.

BUDGETING CORRECTLY

THE RIGHT WAY TO BUDGET

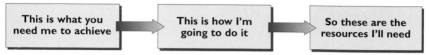

THE WRONG WAY TO BUDGET

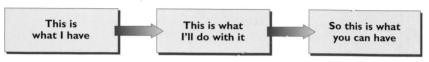

USING TOP-DOWN BUDGETING

Although budgets should be prepared using the output/input method, many managers use the top-down approach (often called "last year's plus"). This very simple method works out what was spent in the previous year and then adds or subtracts a percentage. The flaw in this approach is that the previous year's figures could be wrong, and it is very unlikely to give optimum resource allocations. It may also miss hidden gradual cost changes and can perpetuate inefficient practices. However, top-down budgeting is still the most common way to produce budgeted figures. Often a manager will have had the budget forms in the in-tray for several weeks, and yet, by using this approach, can still produce a budget in one day without reference to any other part of the business.

Q Have I challenged figures and eliminated excess?

Q Where figures have been derived from the top-down approach, is there another way to challenge their validity?

Q Have I met with other managers to discuss their figures in relation to mine?

EXPENDITURE BUDGET

	LAST YEAR	CHANGE	THIS YEAR
Salaries	10,000	6%	10,600
Pensions	1,200	6%	1,272
Motor & travel	500	10%	550
Equipment hire	100	5%	105
Telecom	600	-10%	540
Print, post & stationery	240	-2%	235
Marketing	300	8%	324
Storage	60	3%	62
Maintenance	120	10%	132
Heat, light & power	480	-5%	456
	13,600		14,276

USING THE ▶
TOP-DOWN APPROACH

A listing of all revenue items for last year's actual results or last year's budget should be used as the incremental basis for estimating the figures for this year's budget.

Only items from last year will appear in current year budget

Add or subtract increments to or from last year

USING BOTTOM-UP BUDGETING

60 Introduce bottom-up testing gradually for selected departments.

61 Be sensitive to the concerns that bottom-up cost-cutting can cause.

Consider using bottom-up, or zero-based budgeting (ZBB), which questions the relationship between costs and benefits. State the purpose and outcome of varying expenditure for each activity, starting from a base of nothing (or zero). This means you will have to justify all expenditure, from the ground up. Bottom-up budgeting is best suited for discretionary and support costs, such as marketing costs, rather than tangible costs (easily measurable costs), such as production costs. Bottom-up budgeting is very time-consuming. Some managers prefer not to use it because it is considered to be an aggressive approach.

TOP-DOWN COMPARED WITH BOTTOM-UP BUDGETING

	TOP-DOWN	BOTTOM-UP
STARTING POINT	Last year's budget or actual	Zero: assume no spending at all
BASIS FOR BUDGET	Last year plus or minus a sum	Activity-based building blocks
AMOUNT BUDGETED	Normally a single sum	Range of amounts
NEEDS AWARENESS OF	Individual function/department	Whole of the business
PEOPLE INVOLVED	Manager and owner only	Cross-functional groups
TIME AND EFFORT	Can be significant	Often very substantial
FREQUENCY	Usually annual	Periodically over years
ALTERNATIVES	Only mentioned briefly	Subjected to detailed review
PRIORITIES	Often not stated	Wants and must-haves discussed

ACTIVITY-BASED COSTING (ABC)

To generate accurate figures and gain a better feel for which products and services make money, you must understand what drives the costs in your department. Often, costs are allocated back to each product and service in proportion to sales revenue only. However, this does not take account of other business features, such as office space, head count, and units of product sold. Activity-based costing is a more complete way to understand what drives costs as it allocates each cost in proportion to several business features. By keeping detailed timesheets and cost records for everyone and every activity, you can make a more accurate costing allocation based on the whole organization.

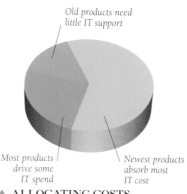

Old products need little IT support

Most products drive some IT spend

Newest products absorb most IT cost

▲ **ALLOCATING COSTS**

Information Technology (IT) costs are driven by newer products that are difficult to support, rather than high volume, easily administered older ones.

QUESTIONS TO ASK YOURSELF

Q Should I introduce zero-based budgeting for certain support departments?

Q Would the "What if?" analysis provide a useful insight to my budgeted amounts?

Q Have I considered obtaining a range of forecasts, instead of working to just a single figure?

62 Use ranges of outcomes to get away from "single figure syndrome."

USING OTHER METHODS

Other ways of testing the figures assess how artificial changes to the budget can affect the outcome. The "What if?" analysis (usually adding 10 percent to key costs and deducting 10 percent from certain revenues) shows up clearly financial sensitivities within the budget. Since budgets typically produce one final figure, such as "Sales will be $15m," you should also consider what might be achievable with favorable conditions, and what might be the worst outcome. By ascribing each single figure outcome a probability, and multiplying the outcome by the probability, a more accurate figure, called the expected value, can by calculated. Calculating a range of best/most likely/worst-case scenarios can help the budget committee decide whether to add one manager's best to another's worst, and so on.

UNDERSTANDING CAPITAL BUDGETS

Expenditures on large capital items such as premises, equipment, and machinery are not included in departmental budgets. Yet assessing capital spending is crucial for your organization's success, so it is vital that you understand capital budgeting.

63 One wrong capital spend can undo all the perfect profit planning.

64 Remember, capital spending is often poorly controlled.

65 Ensure profit-and-loss sheets reflect capital spending.

CONTROLLING CAPITAL

The constraints exerted by organizations over their capital spending can come as a surprise to the inexperienced, yet the price of making mistakes over it can be bankruptcy. Capital spending often takes place early on, and if it is not controlled it can have a domino effect on the rest of the business. Life-sustaining cash can disappear in significant amounts, often on frivolous purchases. Typically, spending overruns the budget, the project starts late, receipts from sales take longer to arrive, and suddenly there is a cashflow problem.

AUTHORIZING CAPITAL

Organizations have developed sophisticated and often long-winded procedures for authorizing capital. Many organizations have a capital-investment committee (which includes senior management) that sets the limits for how much capital can be spent on a project and how the timing of that capital spending is regulated within the organization. There are also capital-approval forms and various other policies and procedures that organizations devise to apply rigorous checks on the authorization of capital spending.

POINTS TO REMEMBER

- An environment should be created that will generate ideas for future capital investment.
- Procedures for authorizing capital must be understood.
- The financial hurdles a project must overcome to be viable should be clearly undersood.
- Acquisition of new assets must be examined using a capital-appraisal method.

ASSESSING PROJECTS

Consider whether capital investment is needed

↓

Assess the risks, and plan how they will be managed

↓

List the tangible and intangible benefits

↓

Write the business case and obtain approval

↓

Carry out the plan, and review project's success

JUSTIFYING CAPITAL SPENDING

To assess the viability of a project, you must justify, in financial terms, how much capital you will have to spend on it. A project can be measured in terms of how many dollars of profit it returns per dollar invested (known as the "return on capital"). A more useful indicator is the "payback period," which is the time taken to recoup the initial investment. However, both these methods fail to take into account the time value of money. We all instinctively know that $1 today is worth more than $1 tomorrow. When looking at future amounts, we should therefore express them in terms of today's value – known as present value or discounted cash flow (DCF). For example, assuming 10 percent interest, $1 in a year's time is worth 91 cents today, and $1 in two years' time is worth 83 cents today. Only discounted cash flow recognizes the time factor, and reduces the real value of future amounts before adding up costs and revenues.

LINKING CAPITAL BUDGETS

Once a capital budget has been authorized, remember that it will have a domino effect to other budgets and will have a profound effect on cash flow. As a result of capital spending on new machinery, for example, the sales budget should reflect the benefits to the organization of the increased capacity or efficiency afforded by the purchase. For costs budgets, apart from depreciation (which is a fixed cost), different assets will influence the type of additional cost incurred. Motor vehicles will increase gas, insurance, and tax costs, whereas buildings will affect utility and maintenance costs.

66 When assessing projects, always consider the "do nothing" option.

67 Be aware that revenue and capital spending are related.

PRODUCING CASH BUDGETS

Cash flow is the movement of money into and out of a business. If you do not have enough cash flow, then your business will be threatened. Create a cash budget to help you predict cash flow over time and to keep an informed eye on your business.

68 Be aware that cash flow usually turns out to be worse than you plan for.

UNDERSTANDING CASH BUDGETS

A cash budget takes figures from a profit-and-loss budget and estimates the timing of income and costs, thus budgeting for actual incoming cash receipts and outgoing cost payments. Just as business health will ebb and flow, so will the demands on cash; yet often the cash needs of a business can seem at odds with the profits generated. A growing business will often have short-term financing problems, whereas a mature declining business can often generate surprising amounts of cash.

▲ CHECKING CASH FLOWS
Producing cash flow forecasts involves the whole business producing realistic and consistent assumptions about timings.

QUESTIONS TO ASK YOURSELF

Q Have the effects of sales tax on cash flow been assessed?

Q Are the timings of receipts realistic, especially for new initiatives?

Q Is the interest that builds up on borrowings realistic?

Q How definite are the capital plans, both amounts and timings?

Q Has there been an increase in trading overseas, on different terms?

Q Will new laws on late payments affect cash flows

69 Always remember the saying, "Profits are vanity, cash is sanity."

DO'S AND DONT'S

✔ Do be sensible about the timings of cash flows; they are often made more difficult by optimistic budgets.

✔ Do ask plenty of "What if?" questions about cash flows, should timings of significant amounts change.

✘ Don't assume that cash flow will not be a problem for you just because it has not been in the past.

✘ Don't assume that everyone will always keep to their terms about payments into or out of the organization.

FILLING IN A CASH BUDGET ▼

Extend the profit-and-loss account items and estimate the likely timings for each item. Add the projected cash flows for each month to indicate cash surpluses or funding requirements.

PREPARING A CASH BUDGET

Prepare a cash budget from the profit-and-loss and balance sheet. Often, an organization has standardized cash flow forecasting forms to make it easier. Working monthly, combine the budget amounts with cash flow timing predictions for each item of revenue and expenditure. Remember to include the one-time events. Repeat the process every time amounts or predictions change.

Annual budgeted profit-and-loss account figures are divided into annual and monthly amounts

Timing of cash flow is estimated for the individual profit-and-loss account items

Actual cash receipts and payments are filled for each month

PROFIT-AND-LOSS ACCOUNT			TIMING PREDICTIONS	CASH FLOWS					
ITEM	ANNUAL	MONTH		JUL	AUG	SEP	OCT	NOV	DEC
Sales	+1920	+160	One month credit	0	+160	+160	+160	+160	+160
Purchases	-720	-60	One month credit	0	-60	-60	-60	-60	-60
Direct labour	-576	-48	Immediate	-48	-48	-48	-48	-48	-48
Rent	-60	-5	One month in advance	-10	-5	-5	-5	-5	-5
Heat, light & power	-48	-4	One month credit	0	-4	-4	-4	-4	-4
Insurance	-12	-1	Six months in advance	-6	0	0	0	0	0
Marketing	-72	-6	One month credit	0	-6	-6	-6	-6	-6
Salaries	-192	-16	Immediate	-16	-16	-16	-16	-16	-16
			Monthly cash flow	-80	+21	+21	+21	+21	+21
PROFIT	+240	+20	Cumulative cash flow	-80	-59	-38	-17	+4	+25

Annual profit is calculated by deducting expenditure from revenue

Monthly figure for total cash receipts and payments is calculated

Cumulative cash flow figure for the period is calculated, representing actual money in the bank

CONSOLIDATING BUDGETS

Once you have prepared your budget you will have to submit it to the budgeting committee so that the master budget can be prepared. In light of what the overall figures look like when consolidated, you may have to amend your budget.

70 Keep to a time-table, especially during the final budgeting stages.

71 Make sure figures are consistently prepared once guidelines are set.

REVIEWING DEPARTMENTAL BUDGETS

Before departmental budgets are brought together you must review your own budget and ensure the following steps were undertaken:
- Limiting factors were correctly identified.
- Relevant background information was gathered.
- Both external and internal influences were recognized and considered.
- Other material sources of information and advice were taken into account.
- Types, amounts, and timing of revenues, expenditures, and significant one-time items were conservatively predicted.

Committee chairperson collates all departmental budgets

Departmental manager submits individual budget

SUBMITTING BUDGETS ▲
Only when you are satisfied that you have extensively reviewed your budget, tested the figures, and made any necessary amendments should you submit it to the budgeting committee.

THINGS TO DO

1. Review your budget
2. Test for consistent preparation
3. Prepare initial draft
4. Send out for amendments
5. Collate amendments
6. Resubmit for approval
7. Submit to committee

GAINING APPROVAL

Submit/resubmit your budget to committee

↓

Committee checks budget for feasibility

↓

Committee specifies amendments

↓

Budget is revised

↓

Committee approves final budget

PREPARING A MASTER BUDGET

A master budget is the summary budget of all the budgets that have been individually prepared by departmental managers. It is a single document that the budget committee prepares to describe the whole organization's aims and expectations for future income, cash flows, and financial status. As with the departmental budgets, the focus will be on key areas, such as sales, production, and finance. The master budget provides information in a summarized form, so that senior management can determine whether the budget is acceptable and can be approved. The master budget should include budgets for profit and loss, balance sheet, and cash flows. The criteria senior management use to approve it will vary with each organization, though they will usually relate to higher level measures, such as adherence to long-term objectives, as well as to traditional shorter-term measures such as profitability, return on capital, solvency, and liquidity.

FOLLOWING THE ITERATIVE PROCESS

If the first draft of the master budget does not meet the expectations of senior management, then it will need to be redrafted. Senior management might insist that fundamental changes are made right away, or they might want to assess the impact of certain progressive changes on the overall plan. Each time this happens, you will have to change figures and again resubmit them for approval. A new master budget will be drafted, which will again be presented to senior management. This process will be repeated until a final plan is accepted. This ongoing redrafting and reapproval is known as the iterative process.

72 Consult with everyone involved over changes to the budget.

73 Record any changes, in case you have to refer to them again.

FINALIZING A BUDGET

Once your budget has been consolidated, the budget committee will be ready to finalize the master budget. Be well prepared for dealing with the committee so that you are in a position to put forward the best possible case for your department.

74 Be efficient by budgeting for only appropriate resources.

75 Be effective by achieving all your stated objectives.

76 Probe the budget by using "What if" scenarios.

REVIEWING THE FIGURES

The budget committee's role is to review the figures and assess their viability. You must be prepared to answer questions such as "What if sales rise or fall more than anticipated?", "How will costs for personnel, purchasing, production, marketing, finance, and administration affect the budget?", and "How will interest, inflation, taxation, duties, and quotas affect the budget?". You will need to decide which factors could affect your budget, in what ways, and whether there are any other circumstances that might be relevant to your department and to the whole organization.

PREPARING FOR THE COMMITTEE MEETING

You should be fully prepared for the budget committee meeting. Make sure you are ready and able to answer the following questions before you attend the meeting.

- Why do you have to attend the committee meeting and how important is it?
- Do you know the role of a budget committee, both generally and in your specific business, and are you aware of who sits on this committee?
- How do you intend to put across the case for your department?
- What follow-up might be required?

POINTS TO REMEMBER

- Develop the skills of interpreting a profit-and-loss account and balance sheet by using relevant financial ratios.
- Make sure that any questions about forecasting budgets have been answered satisfactorily.
- Understand the relevance of the master budget to the budgeting process.
- Make effective personal contributions to the key budget committee meetings.

PARTICIPATING IN BUDGET MEETINGS

As your individual departmental budgets are brought into the negotiation process, they are examined in relation to each other. You may simply not be aware of other plans, conditions, and constraints that could affect what your department has budgeted for. Remember that high level executives will be present at budget meetings, representing the major parts of the organization, as well as the chairperson and accountants. The chairperson advises and liaises with departmental heads and coordinates the final agreements. Accountants are there to assist you in your budget preparation rather than to determine the actual content of all the various budgets.

Factory manager has budgeted for new equipment

Chairperson mediates and finds agreed solution

Accountant identifies there is insufficient cash

FINISHING THE BUDGET

Once the budget committee has agreed on the master budget, all departmental and subsidiary budgets will have been consolidated, comprising budgeted profit-and-loss accounts, balance sheets, and cash flow statements. These documents and the supporting subsidiary budgets are used to plan and control activities for the following year. Your budget will remain the centerpiece of control in your department, linking long- and short-term planning in the overall strategy of the organization.

▲ NEGOTIATING BUDGETS
Participating effectively at budget meetings requires an understanding of the agendas of each member of the budget committee, understanding why they are there, and what they are trying to achieve.

77 Remember, budgets can lose credibility when cuts are announced.

MONITORING A BUDGET

Once you have written the budget, revenues must be achieved and expenditure must not be exceeded. To check this, you should constantly review your budget and adjust as necessary.

ANALYZING DISCREPANCIES

There will always be discrepancies between your budget and actual performance results. To make constructive adjustments for the future, provide for a framework with which to understand and analyze all such discrepancies.

78 Ignore differences that will correct themselves the following month.

79 Allow sufficient time in your schedule to identify any discrepancies.

UNDERSTANDING DISCREPANCIES

It is important to understand why there are discrepancies, no matter how small, between your budget and actual performance. What might seem an insignificant discrepancy to you and your department could be crucial to the whole organization, especially if other departments are also not meeting their budgets. By assessing why discrepancies have occurred, you will be able to ensure that the chances of them recurring are reduced and that future discrepancies are more efficiently anticipated.

THINGS TO DO

1. Give equal weight to monitoring and planning.
2. Decide what is important to monitor in your budget.
3. Allow sufficient time to monitor budgets properly.
4. Arrange to be sent regular financial information.

COMPARING ACTUAL WITH BUDGET

Comparing actual performance with budget is the traditional device used by senior management to measure managerial and business performance. A good business-management system asks questions such as, "Do I have the correct plans in place?" and "How is each part of the business contributing?" A budget managed properly and taken seriously becomes a more forward-looking document that can assist senior management to identify trends, predict year-end results, and avoid any unpleasant financial surprises.

THE CONTROL CYCLE ▶

In order to properly monitor the budget, work through the four actions of this feedback loop. This will ensure you have a reliable control activity built into your budgeting process.

80 Allow time for all four steps of the control cycle.

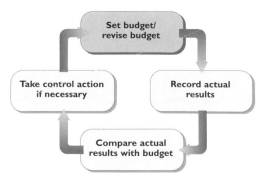

Set budget/ revise budget

Record actual results

Compare actual results with budget

Take control action if necessary

CASE STUDY

For several years, Video Visual had been producing budgets. However, Video Visual's managers found the process of budgeting time-consuming and a significant drain on management resources. Their industry was fast moving and at the leading edge of innovation and technology, and time was very precious to them. As a result they did not make the time to do much with the budget once it had been finalized. They did not monitor what actually happened in the business, and any comparison of actual performance against budget was done only at a very superficial level. Video Visual failed to follow logically the four steps in the control cycle. It learned very little from each year's budget, and so each consecutive year's budget was never likely to be better or more useful to the organization.

◀ FEEDBACK IN ACTION

Making budgeting a learning process need not be time-consuming, but it does require management to assess why figures are not achieved and what might be done in future to correct this. Writing a budget without using it for monitoring purposes is performing only one half of the required task – the two activities go hand in hand.

MONITORING VARIANCES

The discrepancies revealed by comparing actual and budgeted results are called variances, which you must analyze in order to prioritize subsequent action. Overspending is an adverse variance and underspending a positive variance.

81 Define your reporting system when starting the budget process.

82 Prioritize those variances that will be more useful.

83 Use "Flash" reports to define problem areas.

ESTABLISHING PROCEDURES

Continually monitor dicrepancies and understand how they have arisen. Variances are generally categorized as either budget errors or unexpected variances. Constant monitoring helps promote a greater overall understanding of cost behavior, which will help you produce a more accurate budget next time around. However, to do this well, you must establish suitable monitoring procedures. Experience shows that to be truly effective, your procedure must be regular, easy to administer, and sufficiently detailed.

CHOOSING AND MEASURING VARIANCES

Identify significant variances so you can ensure that your budget is adhered to as closely as possible. To select which variances to look at further, consider the likelihood of the variance being controllable, the probable cost of investigating the variance, and the chance that it might arise again in the future. The key question to ask when deciding what to examine is why do you want to look at this variance and, importantly, what will you do with it once it is measured. If it is not going to be of practical use, do not measure it.

QUESTIONS TO ASK YOURSELF

Q What is the procedure for monitoring variances?

Q Are the procedures regular, easily followed, and do they contain sufficient detail?

Q Do the variances measured actually provide useful forward-looking information?

Q Is it realistic to investigate why the variance might have arisen?

Q Are variance reports intelligible and do they contain appropriate comparisons?

UTILIZING VARIANCE REPORTS

There are no rules about how to produce variance reports, and there is no definitive layout. Because variance reports are prepared internally, you can devise any style, though bear in mind that it should be designed specifically to suit your department. Useful reports in one department may well be useless in another. Try to base all reports on the original budget documents to ensure consistency of style. On a practical level managers benefit little from overly elaborate budgeting- and variance-analysis reports. These will be little used because of their complexity, and the result is no improvement in operations. Additional columns are added to show both the price and percentage difference between budget this year and actual last year.

84 Assess the value of your organization's reports to you.

85 To maintain flexibility, include or delete figures as appropriate.

▼ **TYPICAL VARIANCE REPORT**
Whatever the department, a variance report should show items categorized into actual, budget, and prior year sections.

Actual results are compared to budget and expressed as a variance

Heading is month of year of variance report

Actual results are compared to last year's results and expressed as a variance

ITEM	ACTUAL $	BUDGET $	VARIANCE $	%	LAST YEAR $	VARIANCE $	%
Heat	1,200	1,300	100	8%	1,100	-100	-9%
Light	500	550	50	9%	525	25	5%
Telephone	660	700	40	6%	650	-10	-2%
Postage	100	90	-10	-11%	110	10	9%
Stationery	200	180	-20	-11%	160	-40	-25%
Books	50	80	30	38%	50	0	0%
Insurance	240	240	0	0%	220	-20	-9%

DEPARTMENTAL VARIANCE REPORT APRIL YEAR 2

Costs item is described in sufficient detail to help subsequent analysis

Difference betweeen actual results and budget is expressed in dollars

Difference between actual results and last year's results is expressed as a percentage

ANALYZING BUDGET ERRORS

Budget errors occur as a result of poor preparation of the original budget. Sales will be lower than expected while costs will be out of control. It is vital that you understand where you went wrong so that you do not make the same mistakes again.

86 Do not fall for the trap of expecting optimistic income, pessimistic costs.

87 Check all variances; smaller ones might hide larger amounts.

STUDYING THE FIGURES

Actual budget errors may be due to insufficient research into budgeted amounts, a lack of understanding of what drives the business financially, or inadequate challenging of the figures. The obvious solution to low revenues and high costs would be for you to reverse the situation and increase sales while reducing expenditure. But you must analyze why things went wrong and ask yourself the following questions:

● What are the most common variances encountered when monitoring costs, their cause and effects, and possible remedies?

● In particular, what are the main variances in sales revenue, likely causes and effects, and possible remedies?

It can help to understand where errors have crept in by categorizing revenue and expenditure variances into price, volume, and timing.

DISSECTING ERRORS ▲
When analyzing budget errors, concentrate on dissecting the validity and accuracy of the original budgeted amounts.

88 Focus on the root of the problem and do not be overawed by technical variance analysis.

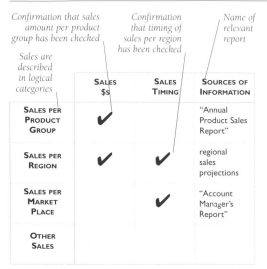

Confirmation that sales amount per product group has been checked

Confirmation that timing of sales per region has been checked

Name of relevant report

Sales are described in logical categories

	SALES $s	SALES TIMING	SOURCES OF INFORMATION
SALES PER PRODUCT GROUP	✔		"Annual Product Sales Report"
SALES PER REGION	✔	✔	regional sales projections
SALES PER MARKET PLACE		✔	"Account Manager's Report"
OTHER SALES			

CHECKING OFF SALES REVENUE ▲

Use a checklist to help investigate the source of errors when predicting sales revenues. It will help to uncover possible explanations in a logical and systematic way.

ANALYZING EXPENDITURE

Use a step-by-step approach to identify expenditure variances. To tackle expenditure queries in a way that is most likely to ensure a successful analysis, ask yourself the following questions:

- Is the price paid for items more or less than budgeted? Is there a cure for this price expenditure variance, and what are the likely financial consequences of the cure?
- Are the amounts purchased more or less than budgeted? Is there a remedy for this volume variance, and what are the possible domino effects of the remedy?
- Is there an expenditure timing difference, can it be fixed, and at what price?

STUDYING INCOME

Though identifying important sales revenue variances is relatively easy, how to remedy them and achieve the original plan is harder and you must keep asking yourself some key questions. First, is there a price variance (selling for more or fewer dollars than expected), what is its impact on the budget, and is there a way to solve it? Second, is there a volume variance (selling more or fewer items than expected), what does it do to the budget, and is there a way around it? Finally, is there a timing variance (not receiving money when expected), and what is its impact on cash flow?

POINTS TO REMEMBER

- All expense types in the cost section of the budget should be checked.

- All sources of income must be tracked – by region, product, market, and salesperson.

- Variances should be categorized into price, volume, and timing to help work out a cure for them.

- Variances should be analyzed in terms of cause, remedy, and the domino effect of the remedy.

- Not all variances have a logical cause or an actionable remedy; some things can just happen.

Investigating Unexpected Variances

There are often cases where a variance could not possibly have been foreseen or avoided. Even though these variances are unexpected there may be something you can do about them and ways that you can learn from their consequences.

89 Do not blame staff for genuinely unforeseeable variances.

90 Only spend time on those variances that you can do something about.

91 Distinguish between poor planning and poor performance.

Avoiding Criticizing Others

One of the main problems with variance analysis is that often a scapegoat is sought when results fall short of plans. Blaming someone for a variance that is effectively unavoidable is very demoralizing. At the time of budgeting there was nothing that the department could, or should, have done differently. Although a variance could not possibly have been foreseen, it may be easily explained with hindsight. So to be more constructive when analyzing unexpected variances you should look beyond apportioning blame and dig a little deeper.

Questions to Ask Yourself

Q Did you define your measurement and variance reporting system when first setting budgets?

Q Have you checked positive variances for opportunities that could be exploited further?

Q Do you combine variance reporting with investigation into causes and possible cures?

Q Have you considered selecting the key variances that are critical to your business?

92 Keep your perspective and do not be drawn into examining variances in too great a detail.

THINGS TO DO

1. Once you have analyzed variances, take action.
2. Investigate favorable as well as adverse variances.
3. Ignore all variance and budgeting alibis.
4. Determine whether a variance is controllable.

93 Remember, foresight is better than hindsight.

STUDYING CONTROLLABLE COSTS

Once unexpected variances have been identified, there may be a lot that you can do about them. A controllable cost is one that can be influenced by the budget holder. If a cost is controllable, then senior management will expect you to exercise your influence and adjust your expenditure where appropriate. Consider the situation where the cost price of a raw material has increased significantly during the budget period. Although you cannot change the price of the raw material, perhaps you could use a cheaper alternative. If skilled labor shortages drive up rates, consider using other grades or even de-skilling the job to avoid this constraint. Using alternatives is not the only type of control you can exercise. You could, for example, consider reducing your discretionary costs by choosing not to spend money on advertising, training, staff parties, and bonuses.

PLANNING AND OPERATING VARIANCES

A meaningful way of looking at unexpected variances is by considering the variance as a planning variance or as an operational one. A typical budget (an ex-ante budget) contains information that was thought to be correct at the time of preparation (ex-ante means "before the event"). An ex-post budget is written after the period to which it relates (ex-post means "after the event"). It is used to produce, with hindsight, the best possible achievable budget. A planning variance is a variance generated by an ex-ante budget that is changed to an ex-post budget. An example of this may be the variance that occurs when an original budget does not take into account a significant increase in raw material price due to a world shortage. This ex-ante budget would be changed to an ex-post budget that builds in this factor for the original time period. An operational variance is where an ex-post budget is compared with actual performance in the current time period. It shows how the department might be currently performing in line with hindsight, which is all that might be reasonably expected.

MAKING ADJUSTMENTS

Having assessed budget variances, you are now in a position to make informed alterations to your budget. The process of comparing actual figures with budget is a continuous one. You should constantly adjust the budget.

> **94** Change your budget to reflect changes in the world.

REFORECASTING BUDGETS

As changes in internal or external factors occur, so actual results begin to diverge from the budget. It can become frustrating for departmental managers when performance reported against budget becomes increasingly less relevant to the actual daily management of the business. It is therefore important that you reforecast the budget periodically (typically quarterly, or at least every six months) to reflect any changing real circumstances.

> **95** Remember that flexing a budget can benefit staff motivation.

KEY ■ Budget result   ■ Reforecast result

▲ JUDGING REALITY

The increasing disparity between the original budget and the latest forecast means that, for monitoring purposes, the original budget has become meaningless and might as well be ignored.

USING FLEXIBLE BUDGETS

A flexible budget takes into account changing real activity. For example, if budgeted sales were 100 units, yet only 80 were sold, in a normal budget all the cost variances would be unfavorable; but this is not particularly informative. A flexible budget, however, shows the expected revenue and expenditure for the actual volume produced and sold (80 units), and so gives a much more valid comparison of real activity against budget.

REVISING A BUDGET

Take great care to ensure that when you amend a budget using flexible budgeting it is as well controlled and structured as the original budget. Often, it is the timing of certain key factors in your budget that give cause for a budget revision. Examples include: change in the timing of sales income, deferral of a new product launch, significant movement in currency rates, new capital investment, unexpected national wage increases. Try and anticipate timing changes and always keep a record of what these changes are so that you can assess their influence on your budget and you can allow for them in future budgets.

THINGS TO DO

1. Revise budgets as soon as necessary.
2. Abandon original budgets if superseded.
3. Have the confidence to change figures.
4. Revise equally rigorously.
5. Measure against flexible budgets.
6. Consider rolling budgets.

96 Ask yourself, "Am I too busy to plan because I do not plan enough?"

ROLLING BUDGET ▼
Budgeting activity for a month is added onto the budget period twelve months into the future, so that, at any time, the budget will stretch twelve months ahead.

USING ROLLING BUDGETS

During a normal annual budget there will come a time when the budget covers only a month or two ahead. Some organizations therefore use a rolling budget, which continuously updates the budget each time actual results are reported, by adding on a further period of budgeting activity. In practice, this involves adding a month or quarter at the end of the existing budget, while dropping off the month or quarter just finished. Be aware, however, that the quality of this type of budgeting is often not the same as a traditional annual budget, because of insufficient time or resources.

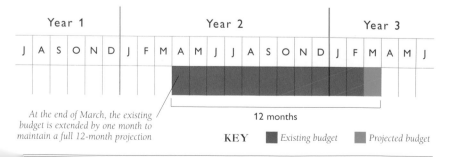

Year 1	Year 2	Year 3
J A S O N D	J F M A M J J A S O N D	J F M A M J

At the end of March, the existing budget is extended by one month to maintain a full 12-month projection

12 months

KEY ■ *Existing budget* ■ *Projected budget*

RECOGNIZING BEHAVIORAL PROBLEMS

As part of the budgeting process, you will have to manage not only financial affairs but also the staff in your department. The success of a budget will depend on the co-operation of all those who are involved in all stages of the budget process.

97 Recognize the human aspects of budgeting, not just financial concerns.

98 Always value the importance of staff motivation to your budget.

ORGANIZING YOURSELF ▼
To use a budget as a key management tool for your department, you must be able to project yourself as a motivator and as an efficient and organized manager.

UNDERSTANDING PEOPLE AND BUDGETS

Be aware that your staff are key to the budgeting process and that inaccuracies in a budget can cause staff demotivation. You should not revise a nonperforming budget by making short-term adjustments that neglect the concerns of your staff. For instance, an easy solution to meeting financial targets would be to reduce discretionary costs, such as staff training, but this results in staff missing out on crucial skill development and could lead to further staff demotivation.

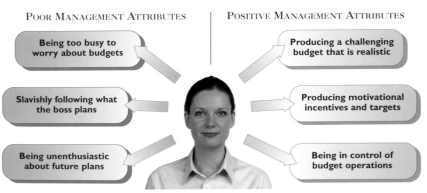

POOR MANAGEMENT ATTRIBUTES

Being too busy to worry about budgets

Slavishly following what the boss plans

Being unenthusiastic about future plans

POSITIVE MANAGEMENT ATTRIBUTES

Producing a challenging budget that is realistic

Producing motivational incentives and targets

Being in control of budget operations

RESOLVING PEOPLE PROBLEMS

Adapt management control systems to meet the differing personalities and attitudes of your staff. Recognize and respond to behavioral issues that arise from using budgets as planning and control tools and you will achieve much better results. Follow these practical solutions:

- Get the best from people by using budgets that are participative and consultative. They are more likely to be successful than ones imposed by senior management.
- Explain to the relevant peope what the budget is all about and exactly what they are expected to achieve and how they are to perform.
- Acknowledge achievement promptly.
- Do not set your targets too high or too low. People can become demoralised when actual results are compared with unattainable budgets. You must judge the correct balance of what is achievable and what is motivational.

CULTURAL DIFFERENCES

The general rule in western countries is that management has to include a motivation factor in its budgets. In countries such as Japan, the focus is more on a co-operative approach to management since motivation is taken for granted. In such countries, being told what to do by management rarely gets the best out of staff.

99 Cultivate accountability with responsiblility.

RECOGNIZING ALIBIS

We have all heard them before – the excuses people use to avoid personal responsibility. It is important to recognize when an excuse is genuine and when it is not, since covering up the truth can result in a poor budget that is not carried out effectively.

ALIBI

I've got demanding clients and problems with suppliers.

I just had to spend everything in my budget this year.

REAL REASON

I'm too busy to produce a meaningful budget and do not value the budgeting process.

I believe that I must spend everything or I will not get as much for my department next year.

BUILDING ON BUDGETING

Some time after your budget has been set and monitored, you should look back over your budgeting activities to learn from your experiences. You should do this after the first three months of your budget and at regular intervals thereafter.

100 Learn from each year's budget so that next year's effort is better.

PREPARING THE BUDGET

Sometimes a budget goes exactly to plan, or at least there are only minor discrepancies that are financially insignificant. Often, however, the differences are more than 10 percent and you should ask yourself why that has happened, starting with the planning phase. Were the advantages and disadvantages of budgeting considered? Did you fully find out about all the types of budget your organization uses and what its budgeting procedures are?

101 Commit yourself to budgeting and you will significantly improve your management performance.

WRITING THE BUDGET

Using hindsight, how well did you do at actually writing the budget? Can you spot any patterns within your budgets? Most companies find that the original budget is hopelessly overoptimistic, the first reforecast is then unduly pessimistic, while the final figures turn out to be close to the target. Assess how can you put your experience into practice in next year's departmental budget. Were certain members of staff persistently inaccurate? Was it more difficult to predict figures for particular products or regions? Was forecasting capital expenditure a major difficulty? Essentially, were you particularly skillful at budgeting, or were you just lucky?

POINTS TO REMEMBER

- Your level of success should be analyzed so that you can plan for greater success next year.
- Budget improvements come only by following a logical and structured model.
- Everyone in the business should be carried along throughout the budgeting process.
- Your appraisal of your own and departmental competence should be honest and frank.
- Budgeting success or failure depends heavily on the people in your department.

LOOKING AT RESULTS ▲
Focus on year-end results, reforecast continuously, and try not to be too proud to learn from your mistakes.

MONITORING THE BUDGET

How well did you monitor the budget? Were your procedural checks and investigations all properly designed and executed so that you knew what had happened when? Could you effectively take the required controlling actions? Perhaps you had deliberately either over- or under-estimated revenues and costs to make results more achievable and expenditure easier to control? Consider the impact of doing this on both your department and the rest of the organization. In doing this, you have probably undermined some of the point of doing a budget in the first place; what should you do differently next time to make sure it does not happen again?

LOOKING TO THE FUTURE

You can manage budgets much more effectively by following a planned procedure and keeping to practical checklists and tips. However, even taking everything into account, things can still go wrong – people, competitors, organizations, and markets are all in a state of constant change. But you must be aware that whatever changes occur, budgeting must go on, and as a manager you must ensure that each year it becomes more effective than ever.

▼ TURNING THE SITUATION AROUND
Just producing a budget is not enough. You must prepare the budget using proper procedures and ensure that everyone understands how it works. Only when everyone is working together can you use the budget as a successful management tool.

CASE STUDY
In their first year Growth.com produced budgets that management did not fully understand. Their first budgeting effort was plagued with problems: everything was late, figures were wrong, and the quality of budgeting in general left a lot to be desired. Senior management were anxious that they should learn from their experiences and that the fiasco should not be repeated in the following year.

They decided to deliver a training program based on the benefits of budgeting. Managers were taught the importance of keeping closely to the timetable, keeping everyone informed and consulted, insisting on high quality figures, and ensuring that the budget was closely and accurately monitored. As a result, the situation was comprehensively turned in the second year and the budget was a great success.

ASSESSING YOUR SKILLS

This very simple questionnaire will help you to evaluate how well you have carried out the budgeting process. The most important part of this exercise is to discover the relationship between what you see as your strengths and your weaknesses. You must be honest with yourself. Check 1 or 4 and only score 2 or 3 where you are in doubt. Add your scores and consult the analysis on page 69. The profile may suggest new avenues for you to explore.

OPTIONS
1 Never
2 Occasionally
3 Frequently
4 Always

1 I plan my department's activities for the forthcoming year in significant detail.

1	2	3	4

2 I am aware of the advantages and the disadvantages of budgeting.

1	2	3	4

3 I prepare for budgeting by understanding its context within the overall business.

1	2	3	4

4 I use budgets as an authority to spend and for judging performance.

1	2	3	4

5 I treat budgeting and its subsequent control as a year-round continuous process.

1	2	3	4

6 I believe in planning for the future no matter how uncertain it might be.

1	2	3	4

7 I communicate plans to my department and listen to their comments and ideas.

1   2   3   4

8 I separate the needs of the organization from my personal ambitions.

1   2   3   4

9 I select a budget model that is relevant to my department.

1   2   3   4

10 I fully appreciate the strengths and opportunities my business possesses.

1   2   3   4

11 I refer to the budget manual and study its contents when I do the figures.

1   2   3   4

12 I understand the role of the budget committee and how it impacts on me.

1   2   3   4

13 I prefer to use standardized budget forms to help get the figures right.

1   2   3   4

14 I use my colleagues' expertise and knowledge throughout budgeting.

1   2   3   4

15 I exhaustively consider how external factors will affect my budget figures.

1   2   3   4

16 I know my department's limiting constraint and how to overcome it.

1   2   3   4

17 I estimate revenues by looking at their likely type, amount, and timing.

| 1 | 2 | 3 | 4 |

18 I check through all last year's expenditure so as not to miss costs.

| 1 | 2 | 3 | 4 |

19 I use my knowledge of fixed and variable costs when predicting future expenditure.

| 1 | 2 | 3 | 4 |

20 I follow the Output/ Input method when I work out the budget.

| 1 | 2 | 3 | 4 |

21 I prefer to budget from a base of zero rather than just adjusting last year's figures.

| 1 | 2 | 3 | 4 |

22 I assess the financial impact of capital expenditure on my department.

| 1 | 2 | 3 | 4 |

23 I understand and use the budgeted case flow forecast for my department.

| 1 | 2 | 3 | 4 |

24 I insist on being included in the iterative consolidating process.

| 1 | 2 | 3 | 4 |

25 I prepare for and participate effectively in budget-committee meetings.

| 1 | 2 | 3 | 4 |

26 I use the four-stage loop: set budget, record actual, compare, and control.

| 1 | 2 | 3 | 4 |

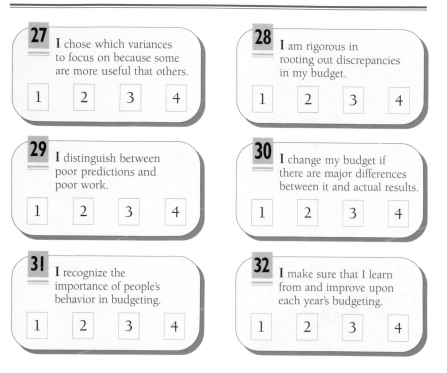

27 I chose which variances to focus on because some are more useful that others.
1 2 3 4

28 I am rigorous in rooting out discrepancies in my budget.
1 2 3 4

29 I distinguish between poor predictions and poor work.
1 2 3 4

30 I change my budget if there are major differences between it and actual results.
1 2 3 4

31 I recognize the importance of people's behavior in budgeting.
1 2 3 4

32 I make sure that I learn from and improve upon each year's budgeting.
1 2 3 4

ANALYSIS

Now that you have completed the self-assessment, add up your total score and check your performance by referring to the corresponding evaluations.

32–63: Your lack of budgeting skills means that you must rethink your approach to budgeting; refer to the relevant sections in this book on the fundamentals regarding your role and best practice in budgeting.

64–95: You have made considerable progress and are reasonably proficient at budgeting. Make renewed efforts to rectify areas of weakness and work on them to get better results from your budgeting.

96–128: You are skilled and competent at budgeting, but do not become too complacent. Remember that your development, like budgeting itself, is a continuous and ever-changing process.

INDEX

A
accountants, budget meetings, 51
activity-based costing (ABC), 43
adjusting budgets, 60–61
alibis, avoiding responsibility, 63

B
balance sheets, 6
  cash budgets, 47
  management accounting
  package, 11
  master budget, 49
  setting targets, 23
balanced business scorecard
  technique, 12
behavioral problems, 62–63
benchmarks, budgets as, 7, 11
bottom-up budgeting, 42
budget period, choosing, 23
budgets:
  adjusting, 60–61
  aims of, 9
  and business strategy, 10–13
  consolidating, 17, 48–49
  defining, 6
  disadvantages of, 9
  finalizing, 17, 50–51
  managing the budgeting
  process, 14–17
  monitoring, 17, 52–65
  potential problems, 18–19
  preparing to budget, 16, 20–29
  standardizing, 24–27
  why budget?, 8–9
  writing, 17, 30–51, 64
business plans, 10–11
business strategy, 10–13, 23
business units, internal
  influences, 32

C
capacity, limiting factors, 33
capital expenditure:
  capital budgets, 44–45
  estimating, 36, 37
  writing a budget, 17
cash flow, 6
  capital budgets and, 45
  cash budgets, 46–47

discounted cash flow (DCF), 45
  management accounting
  package, 11
  master budget, 49
  monitoring, 35
  setting targets, 23
charts, in budget manual, 24
coordination, budget aims, 9
committees:
  capital-investment committees,
  44
  challenging figures, 40
  finalizing a budget, 50–51
  standardizing a budget, 25
  submitting budgets to, 48
communication:
  avoiding problems, 19
  budget aims, 9
community, external influences, 31
compatibility, 28
competitors, external influences,
  31
conflicts of interest, 18, 19
consolidating budgets, 17, 48–49
continuous budgeting, 12–13, 29
control, budget aims, 9
control cycle, monitoring a
  budget, 53
controllable costs, 59
corporate objectives, 23
costs:
  activity-based costing (ABC),
  43
  bottom-up budgeting, 42
  capital budgets and, 45
  controllable costs, 59
  estimating, 36–37
  top-down budgeting, 41, 42
  understanding, 38–39
customers:
  external influences, 31
  monitoring cash flow, 35

D
demotivation, 18
departmental budgets:
  internal influences, 32
  reviewing, 22, 48
direct costs, 39
disadvantages of budgets, 9

discounted cash flow (DCF), 45
discrepancies:
  analyzing, 52–53
  monitoring variances, 54–55
discretionary costs, 62

E
economy, external influences,
  31
errors, analyzing, 56–57
estimates:
  expenditure, 36–37
  revenues, 34–35
evaluation, budget aims, 9
ex-ante budgets, 59
ex-post budgets, 59
expenditure:
  activity–based costing
  (ABC), 43
  analyzing budget errors, 57
  bottom-up budgeting, 42
  capital budgets, 44–45
  estimating, 36–37
  top-down budgeting, 41, 42
  writing a budget, 17
external influences, 30–31

F
figures, producing, 40–43
finalizing a budget, 17, 50–51
fixed costs, 38
flexibility, 28, 29
flexible budgets, 60–61
forecasts:
  cash flow, 46
  reforecasting budgets, 60
forms, 26–27
  in budget manual, 24
  cash flow, 47
  controlling capital budgets,
  44
four step approach, 22
future:
  targets, 29
  uncertainty, 14

G
golden rules, 28–29
government, external
  influences, 31

ACKNOWLEDGMENTS

AUTHOR'S ACKNOWLEDGMENTS

I would like to thank the editors and designers at both Studio Cactus and Dorling Kindersley for the enthusiasm and professionalism they have shown throughout the project.

PUBLISHER'S ACKNOWLEDGMENTS

Dorling Kindersley would like to thank the following for their help and participation:

Editorial Jane Simmonds; **Indexer** Hilary Bird; **Proofreader** John Sturges; **Photography** Steve Gorton, Richard Parsons; **Photographer's assistant** Andrew Komorowski.

Models Roger Andre, Philip Argent, Angela Cameron, Kuo Kang Chen, Carole Evans, John Gillard, Ben Glickman, Richard Hill, Maggie Mant, Frankie Mayers, Chantal Newall, Kiran Shah, Lynne Staff; **Make-up** Nicky Clarke.

Special thanks to the following for their help throughout the series:
Ron and Chris at Clark Davis & Co. Ltd for stationery and furniture supplies; Pam Bennett and the staff at Jones Bootmakers, Covent Garden, for the loan of footwear; Alan Pfaff and the staff at Moss Bros, Covent Garden, for the loan of the men's suits; David Bailey for his help and time; Graham Preston and the staff at Staverton for their time and space.

Suppliers Apple Computer UK Ltd., Cadogan and James, Gieves and Hawkes, Mucci Bags, Positive (Computing), Viper Microsystems.

Picture researcher Andy Sansom; **Picture librarian** Melanie Simmonds.

PICTURE CREDITS

The publisher would like to thank the following for their kind permission to reproduce their photographs:

Key: b=bottom; c=centre; l=left; r=right; t=top
PowerStock Photolibrary/Zefa: 4, 6; **Rex Interstock**: Alexander Caminada front jacket l; **Superstock Ltd**: 36; **Telegraph Colour Library**: Bavaria Bildagentur 56.

AUTHOR'S BIOGRAPHY

Stephen Brookson qualified as a chartered accountant with KPMG and went on to work for Ernst & Young before setting up his own management and training consultancy. He has presented seminars and training events in many countries, and is the author of *Mastering Financial Management*.